MONEY BOX

Making Money

Ben Hubbard
and Beatriz Castro

W
FRANKLIN WATTS
LONDON · SYDNEY

First published in Great Britain in 2019 by
The Watts Publishing Group
Copyright © The Watts Publishing
Group 2019

Credits
Series Editor: Julia Bird
Illustrator: Beatriz Castro
Packaged by: Collaborate

HB ISBN 978 1 4451 6434 2
PB ISBN 978 1 4451 6435 9

Franklin Watts
An imprint of
Hachette Children's Group
Part of The Watts Publishing Group
Carmelite House
50 Victoria Embankment
London EC4Y 0DZ

An Hachette UK Company
www.hachette.co.uk
www.franklinwatts.co.uk

Printed in Dubai

This book is all about money. Why is money important? You can't eat or drink it, but most of us need money to survive. We use money to pay for nearly everything: clothes, electricity, food and water. It is hard to imagine a world without money.

Some people say money makes the world go round.

When we have some money, we have to make choices.
What should we do with our money? We can:

Save it

Spend it

Share it

Or, make more money!

In the following pages, Maya tries to make some
money. Keep reading to see how she does!

Maya and her friends are watching a TV programme about how money is printed.

Every week Maya and her friends get pocket money from their parents. But the pocket money comes with some rules.

Some people have to do chores for their pocket money.

Some are given an allowance to buy things they need.

Others are not allowed to spend their pocket money on sweets.

But what if we want some extra money?

Maya's mum explains that most people have to work to make money. To do this, people usually work for someone else, provide a service or sell something.

Some rich people inherit money and don't have to work at all. But most people work for their money.

Maya likes the idea of selling something to make money. Maya's grandmother tells her that she used to run a lemonade stand when she was young. They sold lemonade to people who walked by.

This lemonade is delicious. How did you make it fizzy?

You're a real entrepreneur. That's someone who sets up their own business to make money.

Maya's teenage half-brother makes some extra money by providing a service for people. He walks his neighbours' dogs while they are at work.

This way the dogs get some exercise and company while their owners are out.

Maya's older cousin makes money by working for someone else. She has a part-time job working in a corner shop after school.

I serve people, stack shelves and generally help out.

Maya has found it interesting to hear about the different kinds of work. Now she needs a job too! Then, one morning, she gets some good news.

Our neighbour Margaret said she could pay you to clean out her garage. But it's a dirty job and will take all weekend.

At first Maya enjoys the work, but it is tiring. Maya also finds it hard seeing her friends having fun outside on the street.

Are you getting much money for this?

Margaret is paying me the minimum hourly wage, which is the legal amount a boss has to pay.

On Saturday afternoon Maya's parents check up on her. Maya is not happy. The garage is cold and it's more work than she first realised. Maya wants to give up.

Cleaning up this garage will take me the rest of my life. I can't do it anymore!

RECYCLING

On Sunday morning Maya wakes up early. She is tired from working in Margaret's garage yesterday, but today she is determined to finish the job.

That night, Maya's dad makes her favourite dinner. Both Maya's parents are very proud that she finished her garage job.

Well done Maya, you stuck with the work even though it was hard.

I wanted to give up, but it gave me a good feeling when the job was done.

At the park the next day, Maya's friends ask her about the money she made. When she tells them, they wish they had spent the weekend working too!

Wow, Maya you're rich!

Does Margaret have any more garages she needs cleaning?

The money is okay, but it'd be better to earn it doing something fun, or exciting like...

...flying into space.

...making discoveries.

...singing in a band.

...speeding round a racetrack.

But for the moment, Maya is happy just being a kid!

29

Quiz

Now you've reached the end of the book, how much do you think you've learned about making money?
Take this test to find out.

1

What is creating coins called?
- a minting
- b hinting
- c sinting

2

What is paper money made with to stop it being copied?
- a zombie marks
- b vampire marks
- c watermarks

3

What is someone who sets up their own business called?
- a an employee
- b an inventor
- c an entrepreneur

4

What do people who earn money have to pay?
- a pax
- b tax
- c fax

5

What is the legal amount a boss has to pay their workers called?
- a the minimum wage
- b the maximum wage
- c the unknown wage

Answers
a, c, c, b, a

Money words

Invisible ink
Ink used for writing that can only be seen under certain conditions, for example under light or when it is made hot.

Minimum wage
The lowest wage that someone is legally allowed to pay a worker.

Mint
To create coins.

Pocket money
Money that some children are given by their parents, often for help with doing household chores.

Recycling
To break down an object, such as a glass bottle, into its basic materials so that it can be used again to make a different object.

Service
To do a particular job or type of work.

Tax
Money that people give to the government to pay for services, such as education or healthcare. Tax is usually taken out of what people earn.

Watermark
A very light design or picture which is put onto paper such as banknotes to make them harder to copy.

Money facts

There's always more to learn about money.
Check out these facts!

- There wasn't any such thing as money 1,400 years ago. Instead, cowry shells from the ocean were used to buy things in China and Africa.

- China was the first country to use paper money, called banknotes, in the 9th century.

- In 1988, Australia became the first country to make their bank notes out of plastic. Australians can go even swimming with their money!

- Many people pay for things with plastic credit cards instead of banknotes and coins. These cards were invented in the US in the 1920s.

- Different countries have different names for their money. Mexico calls its money the peso. In Thailand it's the baht and in Ethiopia, the birr.